JUL 03

KN

The Countries

Wales

Tamara L. Britton
ABDO Publishing Company

visit us at
www.abdopub.com

Published by ABDO Publishing Company, 4940 Viking Drive, Edina, Minnesota 55435.
Copyright © 2003 by Abdo Consulting Group, Inc. International copyrights reserved in
all countries. No part of this book may be reproduced in any form without written
permission from the publisher.

Printed in the United States.

Photo Credits: Corbis, AP/Wide World
Contributing Editors: Kristin Van Cleaf, Stephanie Hedlund
Art Direction & Maps: Neil Klinepier

Library of Congress Cataloging-in-Publication Data

Britton, Tamara L., 1963-
    Wales / Tamara L. Britton.
        p. cm. -- (The countries)
    Includes index.
    Summary: Provides an overview of the history, geography, people, economy, holidays,
and other aspects of life in Wales.
    ISBN 1-57765-759-4
    1. Wales--Juvenile literature. [1. Wales.] I. Title. II. Series.

DA708 .B75 2002
942.9--dc21
                                                                2001045852

Contents

Hylô!

Hello from Wales! Wales shares the island of Great Britain with England and Scotland. The country is a **peninsula** on the western side of the island. Its grasslands and woodlands are home to many types of plants and animals.

The **United Kingdom (U.K.)** governs Wales. In 1997, the Welsh voted to create their own **assembly**. It met for the first time in 1999.

Today, Wales's cities provide a variety of jobs. Many Welsh people work in service industries. They also work in manufacturing and agriculture.

Wales has a long, proud history. Its people have maintained their own **culture**, even after Wales's union with England. The Welsh are working to keep their language and traditions alive.

Hylô *from Wales!*

Fast Facts

OFFICIAL NAME: Principality of Wales (Cymru)
CAPITAL: Cardiff

LAND
- Area: 8,015 square miles (20,759 sq km)
- Mountain Ranges: Snowdonia, Brecon Beacons
- Highest Point: Mount Snowdon 3,560 feet (1,085 m)
- Major Rivers: Severn, Wye

PEOPLE
- Population: 2,946,200 (2000 est.)
- Major Cities: Cardiff, Swansea, Aberystwyth
- Languages: English, Welsh
- Religions: Protestantism, Catholicism

GOVERNMENT
- Form: Constitutional monarchy
- Head of State: King or queen
- Head of Government: Prime minister
- Legislature: Parliament
- National Anthem: "Hen Wlad fy Nhadau" ("Land of My Fathers")
- Flag: Horizontal white and green stripes with a red dragon in the center.

ECONOMY
- Agricultural Products: Wheat, barley, oats, potatoes; cattle, sheep, fish
- Mining Product: Coal
- Manufactured Products: Electronics, food products, optical equipment
- Money: Pound sterling (1 pound = 100 pence)

CARDIFF

Wales's flag

Wales and England use the same currency, the British pound.

Timeline

700s B.C.	Celtic groups begin moving into Wales
55 B.C.	Romans invade Great Britain
A.D. 400s	Roman Empire collapses
500s	Saxon tribes invade Great Britain
800s	King Rhodri Mawr unites Welsh kingdoms; defends Wales from Viking attacks
900s	Wales in confusion; many people try to gain control of the Welsh kingdoms
1066	William of Normandy conquers Great Britain; the Welsh resist
1258	Llywelyn ap Gruffudd names himself prince of Wales
1284	Statute of Wales puts Wales under English control
early 1400s	Owain Glyndwr leads a revolt against England
1536 and 1543	King Henry VIII issues the Acts of Union; Wales becomes a part of England
mid-1500s	The Reformation causes religious conflict in Europe and Britain
1839-1843	Farmers rebel in the Rebecca Riots
1993	Welsh Language Act gives Welsh equal status with English
1997	The Welsh approve the formation of a local Welsh Assembly

History

Farmers and herdsmen were the first residents of Wales. They came to Great Britain from western Europe. Later, the Beaker folk moved to the island from northern Europe. This group brought advanced metalworking skills to Great Britain.

Around the eighth century B.C., Celtic groups began moving into Wales. The Celts had advanced weaving and agricultural skills. They were also warriors who made iron weapons.

About 55 B.C., the Romans invaded Great Britain. They conquered most of Wales by about A.D. 78. But they were unable to conquer all of Wales or Great Britain.

The Celtic religion was led by priests called druids.

Stained glass in Cardiff Castle shows pictures of warriors from the time of the Anglo-Saxons.

The Romans set up towns and built roads. They introduced Christianity to the island. The Romans ruled Wales until their empire collapsed in the early 400s.

After the Romans left, Germanic tribes began invading the island. Around 500, Saxon tribes invaded the land.

About this time, many small kingdoms developed in Wales. These kingdoms fought against Anglo-Saxon groups in the east. In the 700s, the Anglo-Saxons had a king named Offa. He built Offa's Dyke to keep out Welsh invaders. Part of it is still the border between England and Wales.

In the 800s, King Rhodri Mawr (HROHD-ree MOWR) fought against Viking raids. He united some of the Welsh kingdoms for a time. His

The Normans invade Britain

grandson, Hywel ap Cadell (HUH-wehl ap KA-dehl), developed a system of laws for Wales. But in the late 900s, Wales fell into confusion. Many groups tried to gain control of the kingdoms.

William of Normandy conquered Great Britain in 1066. But the Welsh kingdoms resisted Norman rule. In the late twelfth century, Llywelyn ap Iorwerth (HLUHWEHL-in ap YOR-wehrth) briefly unified much of northern Wales.

In the thirteenth century, Llywelyn ap Gruffudd (GRIHF-ihth) again united most of the Welsh kingdoms. In 1258, he named himself the prince of Wales. He signed a treaty with England's King Henry III. But war broke out again in 1277.

King Henry VIII

Llywelyn ap Gruffudd died in 1282. Two years later, the **Statute** of Wales put Wales under English control. Wales became part of England.

In 1400, Owain Glyndwr (OH-ihn GLUHN-door) led a revolt against the English. England lost much control over Wales before 1407. But the Welsh **rebellion** eventually failed.

In 1536 and 1543, King Henry VIII issued the Acts of Union. These acts legally united Wales with England. Wales received a new system of laws, and representation in **Parliament**. English became the official government language.

In the mid-1500s, the **Reformation** made Protestantism Britain's official religion. But most Welsh people still spoke their own language. So the new religious books had to be translated into Welsh. This action helped to preserve the Welsh language.

The Industrial Revolution began in Great Britain in the mid-1700s. Factories and industry grew rapidly. Many Welsh moved to the cities to find work. Towns and cities grew, especially in the north and south.

But the new industries created problems in rural areas. Agriculture became less important, and farmers struggled to get by. Between 1839 and 1843, they **rebelled** in the Rebecca Riots.

The Welsh **economy** improved in the late 1800s. But it suffered a **depression** again in the 1920s and 1930s. Thousands of unemployed Welsh people **immigrated** to other countries. The economy did not improve again until after **World War II**.

In 1979, Welsh voters rejected a **referendum** to create their own government **assembly**. But support for a local government began to increase. In the 1980s, the Welsh developed programs to preserve their language and **culture**. The 1993 Welsh Language Act made Welsh equal to English in business and government.

In 1997, the people approved an **assembly** for Wales. The assembly met in Cardiff for the first time in 1999. It is responsible for issues such as education, health care, and **economic** development. The British **Parliament** still governs Wales in other areas.

Today, the Welsh continue to build their local government. Their culture continues to thrive. The Welsh are working to maintain this culture for future generations.

Britain's Queen Elizabeth II signs the official declaration of the opening of the Welsh Assembly in May 1999.

The Land

The countries of Wales, England, and Scotland make up the island of Great Britain. Wales occupies a **peninsula** on the southwestern side of the island. England lies to the east. The Irish Sea borders Wales on the west and north. The Bristol Channel is to the south.

Wales's land includes mountains, **plateaus** (plah-TOHZ) and hills, valleys, and coasts. The country has two mountainous areas. Snowdonia is in the northwest. The Brecon Beacons mountains are in the south.

At 3,560 feet (1,085 m), Mount Snowdon is the highest peak in Wales.

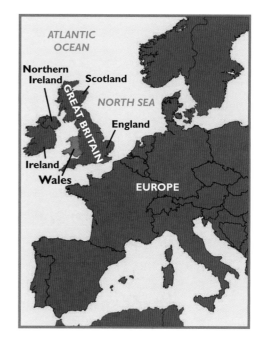

ATLANTIC OCEAN

Northern Ireland

Scotland

GREAT BRITAIN

NORTH SEA

England

Ireland

Wales

EUROPE

Isle of Anglesey

IRISH SEA

SNOWDONIA

Mount Snowdon

Cardigan Bay

Severn River

ABERYSTWYTH

Wye River

BRECON BEACONS

SWANSEA

CARDIFF

Bristol Channel

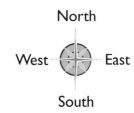

North

West ✦ East

South

Lower **plateaus** and hills surround the mountains. Between the rolling hills are valley lowlands. Two of Wales's major rivers, the Severn and the Wye (WHY), begin in the mountains. They run through the valleys into England or to the ocean.

The coastal regions have high cliffs and flatland areas. Off the northwestern coast is the Isle of Anglesey. It is the largest island in England and Wales.

Wales has a maritime climate. Temperatures in this type of climate are affected by the ocean. The country's winters are mild and summers are cool. Wales receives about 55 inches (140 cm) of rain a year. Snow often falls in the mountains.

The cliffs at North Haven on Skokholm Island have bands of deep pink and purple in the jagged rock.

Rainfall

AVERAGE YEARLY RAINFALL

Inches		Centimeters
Under 40		Under 100
40 - 60		100 - 150

Rain

Temperature

AVERAGE TEMPERATURE

Fahrenheit		Celsius
Over 65°		Over 18°
54° - 65°		12° - 18°
43° - 54°		6° - 12°
32° - 43°		0° - 6°

North

West | East

South

Summer

Winter

Plants & Animals

Wales is made up of grasslands and woodlands. These lands provide homes for many plants and animals.

The Welsh grasslands contain heather, ryegrasses, and mountain grasses. Wales's woodland areas are almost gone due to many years of human habitation. The few remaining forests contain ash, cherry, oak, and maple trees.

Wales's remote landscape has distinctive animals. Bottle-nosed dolphins live in Cardigan Bay. Pine marten and polecats are found in the less populated areas. The European polecat has a long, thin body. Its furry tail is five to eight inches (13 to 20 cm) long.

Many birds nest near the coasts. Manx shearwaters,

The European polecat eats birds, eggs, mice, and fish.

red kites, choughs, and gannets are among the birds that nest there. Gannets are large, white seabirds with black-tipped wings. These birds dive from the air into the water to catch fish.

Wales is working to protect its land and animals. The government has created three national parks. The park at Pembrokeshire Coast protects animals on the mainland and on Wales's many islands. Many of Wales's water birds live on these islands.

A red kite in flight

Brecon Beacons National Park has beautiful mountains, pastureland, and lakes. Hiking, sailing, and caving are popular activities in this park. Snowdonia National Park is a preserve for wild animals and plants. But unlike many national parks, about 26,000 people also live on this land.

Government

Wales is part of the **U.K.** The other countries in the U.K. are England, Scotland, and Northern Ireland. The U.K.'s government is a **constitutional monarchy**.

The U.K. is governed by the monarch and the **Parliament**. Britain's parliament is made up of the House of Commons and the House of Lords. It is led by a **prime minister**. The Welsh people elect 40 members to the House of Commons.

Recently, the Welsh developed the National **Assembly** for Wales. The National Assembly rules from Cardiff. It has taken over many areas of government that used to be the responsibility of the British Parliament.

The Welsh elect 60 members to the Assembly. Forty members are elected directly by the people. The other 20 are chosen based on population.

The National **Assembly** elects the First Minister. This person chooses a **cabinet** of Assembly Ministers. The First Minister and the cabinet lead the National Assembly.

Wales uses the British judicial system. Cases begin in the magistrates' courts, and may move on to the Crown Court. Britain's highest courts are the High Court of Justice and the Court of Appeal in the House of Lords.

Politician Alun Michael addresses the Welsh Assembly on Wednesday, May 12, 1999, during the Assembly's historic first meeting.

Making a Living

In the past, Wales's **economy** was based on agriculture. Today, the Welsh have a variety of employment possibilities available to them.

In the country, many Welsh people are farmers. They grow wheat, barley, oats, and potatoes. Some also raise cattle and sheep. Some Welsh people fish for salmon, trout, cod, and sole.

In the cities, many Welsh people work in service industries. These people work in hospitals, banks, schools, hotels, or restaurants. Many work at coastal resorts in the tourist industry.

The cities provide other jobs, too. Many Welsh people are engineers. Others manufacture goods such as electronics, car parts, and food products.

Much of Wales's electricity is provided by alternative methods. The Welsh use both **hydroelectric** and windmill power.

Welsh farmers commonly raise sheep. These animals are a large part of the Welsh agricultural industry.

Welsh Cities

Most Welsh people live in small villages and towns. But Wales also has beautiful cities. The largest are Cardiff, Swansea, and Aberystwyth (ah-buh-RIS-twith).

Cardiff lies on Wales's southeastern coast. It is the country's capital and largest city. It is also an important seaport. Cardiff's people make cars, mine iron, and produce steel. The city also has flour mills and food processing plants.

Cardiff is known for its civic center and parks. The National Museum of Wales and a **campus** of the University of Wales are also there. Llandaff (HLAHN-dahf) Cathedral and Cardiff Castle are two of the oldest buildings in the city.

The original Cardiff Castle was built around 1091. It has since been added onto and remodeled.

Swansea is Wales's second-largest city. Its people make metal products from nickel, lead, and zinc. The city supplies oil for refineries in other Welsh cities.

The Royal Institution of South Wales and the Glynn Vivian Art Gallery are in Swansea. Its university college has a good reputation in engineering and **metallurgy**. Dylan Thomas, a famous Welsh poet, was born in Swansea.

Aberystwyth is the third-largest city in Wales. This coastal city is a popular vacation spot. It is also considered a main area of Welsh **culture**. The University of Wales began there in 1872. Aberystwyth's National Library of Wales is Great Britain's main copyright library.

The rooftops of Aberystwyth

From Here to There

Wales today has a large network of roads. Many of these highways connect Wales with England. The main land route into Wales is the Severn Bridge. It is part of the main highway that links southern England with South Wales.

Rail travel is still used in Wales, too. Trains connect Welsh cities and towns with each other and Great Britain. Smaller rail lines also have routes through the beautiful countryside.

Wales has no inland waterways. But the Welsh import oil, ore, and other goods through their seaports. **Ferries** link Wales with Ireland.

Cardiff International Airport is the largest airport in Wales. From there, people may travel within the **U.K.**, or to other countries.

To keep the Welsh informed, BBC Wales broadcasts radio and television programs in Welsh and English. Channel Four Wales broadcasts its programs in the Welsh language. The *Western Mail* is the national newspaper. Many people also read Welsh-language community papers.

The Severn Bridge is 3,240 feet (988 m) long. When it was built in the 1960s, it was one of the world's longest suspension bridges.

The Welsh

Most of Wales's citizens are Welsh. Many English people live there, too. Many of these people live in small rural villages or towns. The villages often have only a church, a store, and a **pub**. Small stone cottages and houses surround them.

Wales also has some larger cities. There, many people live in public housing. They rent these types of houses from the government.

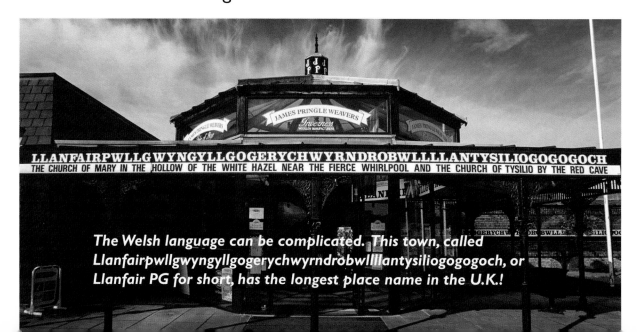

The Welsh language can be complicated. This town, called Llanfairpwllgwyngyllgogerychwyrndrobwllllantysiliogogogoch, or Llanfair PG for short, has the longest place name in the U.K.!

LLANFAIRPWLLGWYNGYLLGOGERYCHWYRNDROBWLLLLANTYSILIOGOGOGOCH
THE CHURCH OF MARY IN THE HOLLOW OF THE WHITE HAZEL NEAR THE FIERCE WHIRLPOOL AND THE CHURCH OF TYSILIO BY THE RED CAVE

JAMES PRINGLE WEAVERS
Inverness
WOOLLEN MANUFACTURERS

Most people in Wales speak English. But there are still some Welsh-speaking areas. Welsh is one of the oldest languages in Great Britain. It is spoken in many public places, including schools. The people have worked hard to keep their language alive.

Most Welsh people follow Protestant religions. They are Methodist, Baptist, or Anglican. There are many Roman Catholics, too.

The Welsh have many traditional foods. People still eat *cawl* (COWL), laver bread, *bara brith* (BAH-rah breeth) fruit bread, and Welsh cakes. *Cawl* is a light soup with lamb meat. Laver bread is actually a red seaweed cooked with oatmeal and served with bacon.

A Welsh butcher stands in front of his shop.

Conwy Castle is one of many medieval castles that still stand in Wales today.

Welsh children between the ages of 5 and 16 must attend school. Students learn a variety of required subjects, including the Welsh language. After secondary school, students may go on to colleges, universities, or **vocational** schools.

Caws Pobi

Caws Pobi, or Welsh Rarebit, is an old Welsh recipe.

- 6 cups shredded cheddar cheese
- 3/4 cup milk
- 2 egg yolks, beaten
- 1/8 teaspoon cayenne pepper
- 1 teaspoon Dijon mustard
- 1 teaspoon salt

Melt the cheese in a double boiler. Mix egg yolks, milk, pepper, and mustard in a small bowl. Add to melted cheese. Stir until heated through. Serve on toast.

AN IMPORTANT NOTE TO THE CHEF: Always have an adult help with the preparation and cooking of food. Never use kitchen utensils or appliances without adult permission and supervision.

English	Welsh
Yes	Ie (YEH)
No	Nage (NA-ga)
Thank you	Diolch (DEE-ohlkh)
Please	Os gwelwch yn dda (os GWEHL-ookh uhn thah)
Hello	Hylô (HI-loh)
Good-bye	De boch chi (deh BOKH khee)

LANGUAGE

Holidays

The Welsh celebrate many holidays. They begin the year with New Year's Day, on January 1. This day is usually celebrated with friends.

On March 1, the Welsh celebrate St. David's Day. This holiday honors St. David, the patron saint of Wales. The Welsh often wear leeks and daffodils, as well as their traditional clothing, on this day.

In the spring, Easter is spent with family. The Welsh attend church, color Easter eggs, and eat together. Often, Easter meals include hot cross buns.

In July, the International Music Festival features many types of music. In August, the Welsh celebrate their most important festival of the year. The Royal National *Eisteddfod* (ay-STETH-vawd) of Wales is a national **cultural** festival. It features Welsh-language music, poetry, drama, and arts.

Opposite page: Young girls perform in a druid ceremony at the Eisteddfod festival.

In the fall, people attend the Swansea Festival of Music and the Arts. At the end of the year, Christmas is celebrated with family. Many families go to an early morning church service. Later, they exchange gifts and eat a big meal.

Sports & Culture

The Welsh play many sports. People in Wales commonly play rugby, soccer, cricket, and baseball. Rugby is popular throughout Britain. In the Six Nations Championship, Wales plays England, Ireland, Scotland, France, and Italy for the top rugby title.

Welsh people also enjoy many outdoor sports. Hiking, climbing, and sailing are popular activities in Wales's three national parks. Golf is also widely played throughout Wales.

Welsh athletes have won awards for their talent. Colin Jackson and Iwan Thomas have won medals for hurdles and track at world championships and the Olympics. Tanni Grey-Thompson has won gold medals for wheelchair racing at the Paralympics and other marathon races.

Colin Jackson placed fifth at the 2000 Olympics. He currently holds the world record for hurdles in the 110-meter category.

Welsh **culture** also includes the arts. Literature has long been a part of the Welsh tradition. An example is *The Mabinogion,* a collection of mythical Welsh tales.

In the early 1900s, William John Gruffydd wrote poems in the Welsh language. But the best known Welsh poet is Dylan Thomas. He wrote many poems, along with the famous play, *Under Milk Wood.*

In the movies, Welsh films have won many awards. Some Welsh actors are known around the world. Richard Burton, Anthony Hopkins, and Catherine Zeta-Jones are award-winning Welsh actors.

The Welsh are also well known for their men's choirs. Church services often involve singing hymns. Welsh hymns are often accompanied by harp music. The triple harp is Wales's national instrument.

The Welsh have a strong cultural identity. Despite the country's union with England, the Welsh language, traditions, and arts have survived. The Welsh people continue to take pride in their country and culture.

One of Dylan Thomas's most famous poems is "Do Not Go Gentle into that Good Night."

Glossary

assembly - a group of government officials who make and discuss laws.

cabinet - a group of advisers chosen by the First Minister to lead government departments.

campus - the grounds and buildings of a university, college, or school.

constitutional monarchy - a form of government ruled by a king or queen who must follow the laws of a constitution.

culture - the customs, arts, and tools of a nation or people at a certain time.

depression - a period of economic trouble when there is little buying or selling and many people are out of work.

economy - the way a city or nation uses its money, goods, and natural resources.

ferry - a boat used to carry people, goods, and cars across a body of water.

hydroelectric - electricity produced by water-powered generators.

immigrate - to enter into another country to live.

metallurgy - the science and technology of working with metals.

parliament - the highest lawmaking body in some governments.

peninsula - land that sticks out into water but is connected to a larger land mass.

plateau - a raised area of flat land.

prime minister - the highest-ranked member of some governments.

pub - short for public house. A place in the U.K. that serves food and drink where people often meet to socialize.

rebellion - an armed attack on a government.

referendum - a direct vote by the people on a public matter.

Reformation - a religious movement in the sixteenth century. People wanted to reform the Catholic Church. They formed Protestant churches by making these changes.

statute - a law established by the legislative branch of a government.

United Kingdom (U.K.) - the united countries of England, Scotland, Wales, and Northern Ireland.

vocational - of or relating to training in a skill or trade to be pursued as a career.

World War II - 1939 to 1945. Fought in Europe, Asia, and Africa. The United States, France, Great Britain, the Soviet Union, and their allies were on one side. Germany, Italy, Japan, and their allies were on the other side. The war began when Germany invaded Poland.

Web Sites

Would you like to learn more about Wales? Please visit **www.abdopub.com** to find up-to-date Web site links to more information on the castles of Wales and the British monarchy. These links are routinely monitored and updated to provide the most current information available.

Index